Bead stringing

These are the key tools and findings you'll use to make professional-quality jewelry.

Findings

"Findings" are the parts that link beads into jewelry. Buy the best metal findings you can afford. Base metal will eventually discolor, but sterling silver and gold-filled findings are surprisingly affordable.

A. A *head pin* looks like a blunt, long, thick sewing pin. It has a flat or decorated head on one end to keep the beads from falling off. Head pins come in different sizes.

B. *Eye pins* are just like head pins except that they have a round loop on one end. You can make your own eye pins from wire.

C. A *jump ring* is used to connect two loops. It is a wire circle or oval with a split.

D. *Split rings* are more secure than jump rings. They look like tiny key rings and are made of springy wire.

E. *Crimp beads* are large-holed, thin-walled metal beads designed to be flattened. You use them instead of knots when stringing on flexible beading wire.

F. *Bead tips* are small metal container beads used to link a cord-strung necklace to a clasp and conceal the knots. They come in either a basket shape or a two-sided, open bead shape. You squeeze the halves of the bead type together with the knot inside.

G. *Clasps* come in many sizes and shapes including: a toggle, consisting of a ring and a bar; a lobster claw or spring ring, which open when you push on a tiny lever; an S-hook, which links two soldered or split rings; and a hook and eye.

H. *Earrings* come in a huge variety of metals and styles, including post, French hook, kidney wire, and hoop. A loop on earring findings lets you attach beads.

I. *Cones* are ideal for concealing the ends and knots of a multi-strand necklace and joining it to the clasp.

Tools

You need very few tools for making bead jewelry, but don't use the large, grooved pliers in your family tool kit.

J. *Chainnose pliers* for jewelry making have smooth, flat inner jaws, and the tips taper to a point so you can get into tiny spaces. Use them for gripping and for opening and closing loops and rings.

K. *Flatnose pliers* don't come to a point at the tip, so they can't go everywhere that chainnose pliers can. They are useful but not necessary.

L. *Roundnose pliers* have smooth, conical, tapered jaws. You form loops around them.

M. On *diagonal wire*

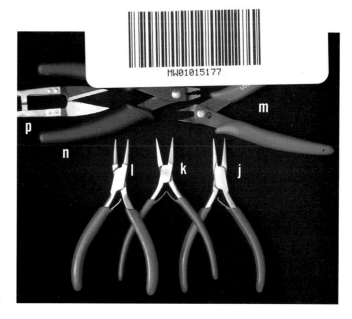

cutters, the outside (back) of the blades meets squarely yielding a flat-cut surface. The inside of the blades makes a pointed cut. Always cut wire with the back of the blades against the section you want to use. Do not use jewelry wire cutters on memory wire, which will ruin them; bend memory wire until it breaks.

N. If you use crimps often, you'll want *crimping pliers*. These have two grooves in their jaws to fold a crimp into a tight cylinder.

O. An *awl* is the easiest tool to use when knotting between beads.

P. Use *thread snips* for cutting bead-stringing cord. Medium-weight, fine-pointed scissors or clippers are ideal.

Q. *Twisted wire needles* are made from a length of fine wire folded in half and twisted tightly. They have a large eye at the fold, which is easy to thread. The eye flattens when you go through beads.

Stringing materials

Flexible beading wire comes in several brands. All consist of very fine wires twisted or braided together and covered with a smooth plastic coating. Aculon (tiger tail) is the stiffest and will kink easily because it only has 7 inner wires. Soft Flex and Beadalon comes in colors and have many inner wires (21 or 49). They drape well and are relatively kink resistant.

Cord is the most common stringing material. It consists of several plied (twisted) finer cords. Nylon is the most common material for bead cord. Cord size is indicated either by a number or a letter; the lower the number or letter, the thinner the cord, except for O, which is very thin. Choose a size that will pass through your beads snugly four times, and always string with doubled cord. Pearls are traditionally strung on silk, but many of the new nylons are almost as supple. Nylon upholstery thread works well too. Do not string beads on monofilament fishing line – it becomes brittle – and sewing thread is too weak.

Wire is used to make loops and eye pins or to wrap beads creatively. The smaller the gauge number, the thicker the wire.

MemoryWire is steel spring wire; it's used for coil bracelets, necklaces, and rings and comes in small, medium, and large coils.

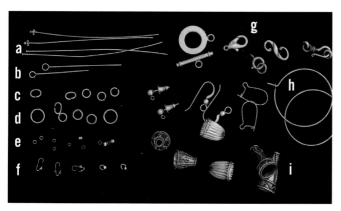

Bead stringing
Earrings: Projects 1&2

You make this basic earring with a head pin and a few beads. Use an eye pin and add a dangle for increased complexity and movement.

Making loops or eyes

Figure 1: Cut the wire, leaving a ⅜-in. (1cm) tail above the bead. Bend it against the bead at a right angle with the tip of a chainnose pliers.

figure 1

Figure 2: Grip the very tip of the wire in roundnose pliers. If you can feel it, the loop will be teardrop-shaped.

figure 2

Figure 3: Without pulling, rotate the wire into a loop as far as your wrist will turn. Let go, regrasp the loop at the same place on the pliers, and keep turning to close the loop. The closer to the pliers tip you work, the smaller the loop.

figure 3

Opening and closing loops

To open a loop, use one or two pairs of pliers to grasp the wire at the opening. Pull one plier toward you and push the other away to separate the ends by moving them out of plane. Never spread the loop side to side; this fatigues the metal. Close the loop the same way.

Project 1:
Basic head pin earring

materials

- **1** Pair French hook findings
- **2** 6mm Amethyst beads
- **4** 2 x 4mm Peridot rondelles (disk-shaped beads)
- **2** Head pins

Tools: chain- and roundnose pliers, wire cutters

stepbystep

❶ Stack a peridot rondelle, an amethyst, and another peridot on a plain head pin.
❷ With the flat side of your wire cutter blades toward the beads, cut the head pin, leaving ⅜ in. (1cm) of wire above the beads for a loop.
❸ Use chainnose pliers then roundnose pliers to make a loop right against the bead, as shown at left.
❹ Open the loop as shown at left and attach it to the loop on the earring finding; then close it. Make the other earring (**photo a**). ●

Project 2:
Adding a joint to the basic earring

materials

- **1** Pair gold French hook findings
- **2** 2-3 in. (5-8cm) Gold eye pins
- **2** 20mm Brass dragonfly charms
- **2** 8mm Green/gold glass beads
- **2** Matte transparent lime size 8º seed beads
- **4** 5 x 2mm Brass fluted rondelles

stepbystep

If the bead elements in an earring are short, you can use one eye pin for two pieces.
❶ String a rondelle, an 8mm bead, and a rondelle on an eye pin. Cut off the excess wire as in step 2 above and set it aside. Make a loop against the second rondelle.
❷ Make a loop at one end of the leftover piece of eye pin wire.
❸ String one 8º seed bead and cut off the excess wire, leaving ⅜ in. (1cm). Make another loop as close to the seed bead as possible.
❹ Open one of the loops on the seed bead wire and string on the charm. Close the loop. Open the other loop and hang it from a loop on the bead and rondelle piece. Close the loop tightly.
❺ Open the other loop on the rondelle piece and hang it from the earring finding's loop. Repeat for the other earring (**photo b**). ●

a   b

Bead tips are the easiest way to begin and end a necklace, join a clasp, and conceal knots in one step.

Project 3: Necklace strung on cord

materials

- **1** Silver clasp
- **2** Silver bead tips
- 2 yd. (1.8m) Size E or F nylon bead cord
- **9** 13 x 7mm Silver-plated beads
- **61** 2 x 4mm Peridot rondelles
- **44** 6mm Amethyst beads
- **21** 5 x 2mm Fluted glass rondelles

Tools: chain- and roundnose pliers

stepbystep

❶ Measure a piece of cord three times the desired finished length of your necklace. Thread on a twisted wire needle and pull it to the center of the cord.

❷ Bring the two ends together and tie a large over-hand knot (**see knots, p. 19**) near the end of the doubled strand (you may need to double or triple it). Seal the knot with clear nail polish or G-S Hypo Cement (**p. 11**).

❸ When the glue is dry,

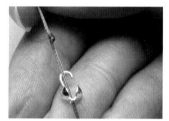

c

d

e

f

string the cord through the bead tip from inside the open bead or basket to the outside (**photo c**).

❹ Then string all the beads in the order you've determined. An inexpensive necklace design board (from a craft or bead store) is a great help for planning a necklace (**see p. 6, photo i**).

❺ Finally, string the second bead tip, entering it from the outside (bottom) of the open bead or basket. Cut off the

needle and tie the two cord ends together with 2-3 square or surgeon's knots (**p. 19 and photo d**). Make sure this bulky knot is too big to pull through the bead tip, then glue it. When the glue is dry, trim the ends and close the bead tips with chainnose pliers (**photo e**).

❻ Attach the ring or eye on each half of the clasp to the bead tip hook by closing the hook around the eye with roundnose pliers (**photo f**). ●

small cylinder (**photo h**). You can also mash a crimp flat with chainnose pliers. Always squeeze whichever tool you use hard enough to keep the wire from slipping.

❸ String all the beads in the order you've planned (**photo i**), making sure that the first 4-8 beads go over the wire tail as well (**photo j**).

❹ After stringing the beads, string another crimp and the other half of the clasp. Bring the wire tail back through the crimp and a few of the end beads. Pull the wire taut so it is snug but does not buckle the beads. Then crimp.

❺ Cut off the excess wire right against the bead it exits, using wire cutters. ❂

g

h

i

j

Bead stringing
Necklace: Project 4

Flexible beading wire supports heavy or rough beads securely. But instead of tying knots, you fasten it around the clasp ends with small, metal crimp beads.

Project 4: Strung on flexible beading wire

materials
- 32 in. (81cm) Flexible beading wire, size .012-.019
- **1** Gold S-hook clasp with 2 rings
- **2** Gold crimp beads
- **46** 8mm Green/gold glass beads
- **5** 19 x 11mm Fluted gold/ivory Czech glass beads
- **8** 6mm Gold-lined clear fire-polished crystals
- **4** 15 x 5mm Pale yellow square glass tube beads
- **64** 5 x 2mm Brass fluted rondelles (disk beads)

Tools: crimping or chainnose pliers, wire cutters

stepbystep

When you use flexible wire for stringing a necklace, you need to secure the ends and attach the clasp with crimps. Flatten crimps with chain-nose pliers or fold them with crimping pliers.

❶ Use beading wire 6-8 in. (15-20cm) longer than the desired finished necklace. Thread a crimp on one end of the wire then bring the end through the loop on one side of the clasp. Take a 3-in. (7.5cm) tail back through the crimp and tighten the space between crimp and clasp.

❷ Crimping pliers have two grooves on the jaws. First, mash the crimp in the groove shaped like a quarter moon to produce a fold groove (**photo g**). The two wires should be on opposite sides of the fold. Following up with the round groove nearer the tip completes the fold, bending the crimp into a

Project 5: Multi-strand necklace with cones

materials

- 1 Hank, size 11° seed beads
- 1 Centerpiece bead – ours was made by Tom Boylan (*B&B* #10)
- 2 10mm Silver Bali beads
- 1 Spool silamide thread or size 0 nylon bead cord
- Size 10-12 beading needle
- 2 Silver cones ¾-⅞ in. long (2cm)
- 8 in. (20cm) 18 or 20-gauge Silver wire
- 1-in. (2.5cm) Silver S-hook clasp with two 6-7mm rings
- G-S Hypo Cement

Tools: chain- and roundnose pliers, wire cutters

stepbystep

❶ String all 11 strands on doubled cord, taking each through the centerpiece bead(s). Leave about 6 in. (15cm) of cord at each end.

❷ Adjust all the strands on one side to the same length and tie them together with an overhand knot tight against the beads (**p. 19**). Repeat at the other end.

❸ Cut two 4-in. (10cm) pieces of wire. Make a wrapped loop, starting an inch from the end of each wire, see **top right**.

❹ Working with one tied end of the necklace, thread half the cords through the loop from one direction and the other half through the other way so they cross (**photo k**). Tie them with a surgeon's knot or two square knots (**p. 19**) and glue the knot. When dry, trim the ends to about ¼ in. (6mm).

❺ Feed the long end of the

Wrapped loops require practice — expect to make at least 15 bad ones with inexpensive copper wire or head pins before you start making consistently good wrapped loops — but they're worth mastering. Not only do they increase security for your beads, they also add a designer touch. You can make one wrap or as many as you wish for the desired effect.

Figure 1: Leaving a ¾-1 in. (2-2.5cm) tail, place the tip of a chainnose pliers where the bead will be. Bend the tail to form a right angle.

Figure 2: With roundnose pliers, grasp the tail just past the bend and pull it over the jaw to point the other way.

Figure 3: Rotate the pliers so the empty jaw is above the partial loop and continue pulling the tail around the bottom jaw until it's perpendicular to the bead or the wire.

Figure 4: Pull a split ring, chain, etc., from the tail into the loop.

Figure 5: To keep the loop round, grasp it with roundnose pliers in your non-dominant hand just above the cross. Don't dent the wire.

Figure 6: Grasp the tail with chainnose pliers and pull it around the wire until it meets the bead. Make the first wrap against the pliers and keep wraps close. Clip.

wire into the cone, exiting the narrow end, and pull the loop up into the cone until it fits snugly inside (**photo l**). For a plain loop, trim the wire to ⅜ in. and make another loop against the top of the cone, or make a wrapped loop around one ring of the clasp (**photo m**). Repeat steps 4 and 5 at the other end of the necklace. ◗

Bead stringing

Necklace: Project 5

Use cones at the ends of a multi-strand necklace to hide the ends and knots professionally.

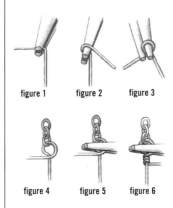

figure 1   figure 2   figure 3

figure 4   figure 5   figure 6

k

l

m

Wire work
Necklace: Project 6

Link beads together on wire, using wrapped loops for a stylish chain.

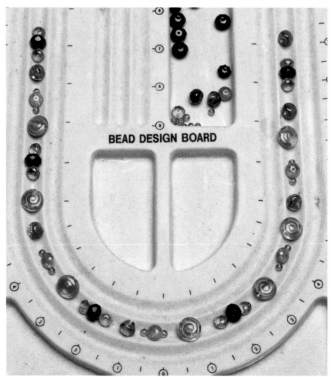

Project 6: Wrapped loop necklace

materials

- Assortment of glass, stone, metal, etc. beads in various shapes and sizes that look good together, about 12 in. (31cm) when strung end to end
- 1 Spool Color Craft or Artistic wire in a complementary color, 22 gauge
- 1 Clasp

Tools: wire cutters, chain- and roundnose pliers; bead design board optional

stepbystep

Wrapped loops add design flair to a necklace or bracelet of linked beads. They also add security. If you use plain loops, a little tug can break your jewelry. Practice making wrapped loops (**p. 7**) with scrap wire before starting the necklace.

Color is an important consideration in designing any piece of jewelry. It's always safe to use shades of the same color, but a necklace in only one color family can look dull or predictable. If you want to be a little daring, choose a small quantity of accent color beads that are opposite your main color beads on a color

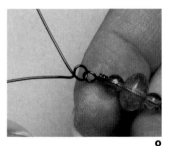

o

p

n

wheel. For example: a little soft orange makes a blue necklace sing; add a dash or green or yellow to a red necklace; or try a hint of purple with a green necklace or vice versa.

Also vary the sizes and shapes of the beads you choose to give the necklace more texture and vitality.

❶ Arrange the beads on a bead design board or a terrycloth towel, leaving almost ½ in. (1.3cm) between each bead or small group of beads (**photo n**). This space will be occupied by the wire loops that join the beads.

❷ Cut a piece of wire for each bead or group of beads that's about 3 in. (7.6cm) longer than the bead(s).

❸ Start working in the center of the necklace. Make a wrapped loop at one end of the wire for the center bead, string the bead, and make a wrapped loop on the other side of the bead.

❹ Start a wrapped loop through figure 3 (don't wrap it) on the next piece of wire. Link the unwrapped loop to the adjacent wrapped loop on the center bead and complete the wrap (**photo o**). String the bead(s) and make a completed wrapped loop on the other side.

❺ Repeat step 4 on the other side of the center bead.

❻ Repeat steps 4 and 5 for each group of beads on both sides of the necklace. Do not wrap the last wrapped loop before the clasp.

❼ Attach the clasp parts to the last loop on each end of the necklace before wrapping (**photo p**).

Alternatively, you can make the necklace long enough to go over your head and link the end loops, omitting the clasp. ◗

Project 7: Beaded bead

materials

- Wooden beads with large holes
- Beading thread, Nymo D or Silamide
- Beading needles, #12
- 2-5g Seed beads, size 11º for each bead 12mm or larger
- Small piece cellophane tape such as Scotch brand
- Clear nail polish or G-S Hypo Cement

Optional: acrylic paint in seed bead color

This easy beaded bead technique gives beautiful results. The trickiest part is keeping beads out of the wooden bead's hole.

stepbystep

If desired, color the wooden beads by rolling them in acrylic paint before beading. Silver is good if you're using silver-lined seed beads, or choose a color that will blend harmoniously with the seed beads you've chosen.

❶ Cover the holes of the bead with small pieces of cellophane tape to help you keep beads from falling inside. Thread 2 yd. (1.8m) of thread on a needle. Go through the hole of the wooden bead and tie the thread tightly around the bead with a surgeon's knot or a square knot or two (**p. 19**). Pull the knot to the edge of the hole and dot it with nail polish or glue.

❷ String enough seed beads to reach around the outside of the bead from hole to hole. Go through the hole of the wooden bead, making sure no seed beads slip inside by keeping the thread under tension at all times.

❸ Repeat step 2 around the bead 10-20 times (depending on the size of the wooden bead). Space the wraps

q

r

s

evenly until beads completely ring the holes. There will be gaps between bead strands at the fattest part of the bead (**photo q**).

❹ String shorter lengths of beads to fill in the gaps, pulling the bare thread down between the beads at the hole so it doesn't show (**photo r**).

❺ To end the thread, take it through a few beads and tie a half-hitch knot (**p. 19**). Repeat at least 3 times. End by going through a few seed beads before cutting the thread.

❻ To use a beaded bead as a button (optional): If the hole opening is large, backstitch seed beads to the threads at the hole one bead at a time (**photo s**). When you have ringed the hole, go through all the backstitched beads again. Then end the thread as in step 5. ◗

Stitches
Beaded bead:
Project 7

You can use a small beaded beads for a button-and-loop closure on a necklace or bracelet. Make larger beaded beads to string for a necklace.

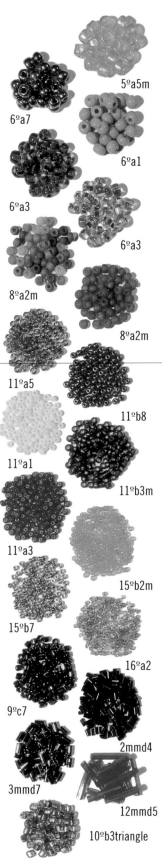

5ºa5m

6ºa7

6ºa1

6ºa3

6ºa3

8ºa2m

8ºa2m

11ºa5

11ºb8

11ºa1

11ºb3m

11ºa3

15ºb2m

15ºb7

16ºa2

9ºc7

2mmd4

3mmd7

12mmd5

10ºb3triangle

About seed beads

Glass seed beads are often perfect for strung necklaces (**see p. 7**). You can use them as spacers on each side of a large bead to make it stand out, or you can string them in groups as part of a necklace's design. But they come into their true glory when you weave or embroider them.

Seed beads come in packages, tubes, or hanks. A standard hank contains twelve 20-in.-long (51cm) strands, but vintage hanks are often much smaller. Keep hanked beads on the hank so you can transfer them easily in groups to the bead thread. Remove a strand at a time to use the beads one by one.

Seed beads have been manufactured in **many sizes** from the largest, 5º (also called E beads), which are about 5mm wide, to teeny size 20º or 22º, which aren't much larger than grains of sand. The larger the number, the smaller the beads. Beads smaller than Japanese 15ºs have not been made for about 100 years. The most commonly available size in the widest range of colors is 11º. (The symbol º stands for aught or zero. The greater the number of aughts, i.e., 22º, the smaller the bead.)

Seed bead finishes can be either **matte (m)** or **shiny** and include **opaque (1)**, a solid colored glass that's popular for Native American beadwork. **Transparent (2)** beads are made of colored glass through which light can pass. They can also be **lined (3)** with colored glass or a colored, dyed, or painted lining. **Silver- or gold-lined** seed beads are lined with real silver or gold. (Most Czech silver-lined seed beads have square holes.) Transparent and some opaque beads may also be

treated with a variety of coatings. These include **iris (4)** or **aurora borealis (AB)** or **luster (5)**, which give multi-colored effects; **opalescent** or **pearlized (6)**; **metallic (7)** (colored metal is fused to the glass surface); or **galvanized (8)** (a rich but impermanent metallic coating). Artist Virginia Blakelock recommends testing beads for colorfastness by washing, rubbing, and putting them in sunlight, nail polish remover, or bleach.

The best **round** seed beads are made in Japan and the Czech Republic. **Czech seed beads (a)** are usually more irregular and rounder than **Japanese seed beads (b)**, which are a bit squared off.

Czech beads give a bumpier surface when woven, but they reflect light at a wider range of angles (silver-lined Czech beads usually have a square hole, which increases their sparkle). They can also fill different sized spaces more easily. The rounder shape makes them ideal for right-angle weave (projects in *B&B* #20, 22, 36, and 43).

Japanese seed beads produce a uniform surface and texture. Japanese and Czech seed beads can be used together, but a Japanese seed bead is slightly larger than the same size Czech seed bead.

Seed beads also come in a sparkly **cut (c)** version. Japanese beads are formed with six sides and are called **hex-cut** or hex beads. The cuts on Czech beads are less regular, and they are usually called **2- or 3-cuts**. **Charlottes** have an irregular facet cut on one side of the bead.

Bugle beads (d) are thin glass tubes. Size 1 bugles are about 2mm long, but bugles are made even longer than 30mm. They can be faceted or hex cut, straight, or twisted.

But selection of colors, sizes, shapes, and finishes is limited.

A new kind of seed bead was invented late in the 1980s by Mr. Masayoshi Katsuoka of Miyuki Shoji Co. The generic term for this bead is **Japanese cylinder bead (e)** (see **p. 11**), but you will hear it called **Delica** (the Miyuki brand name), **Antique or Toho Antique**, or **Magnifica** (the brand names of Toho and Matsuno). Japanese cylinder beads come in hundreds of colors and finishes, including **plated with high-karat gold (9)**. Cylinder beads are extremely popular for peyote-stitch projects, such as amulet purses, since they are very regular and have extremely large holes. They fit together almost seamlessly, producing a smooth, fabric-like surface.

The bead is labeled size 11º, but it is about the size of a Czech 12º – if you want to use it with round seed beads. In the mid '90s, Toho began making the **3.3 cylinder bead (f)**, so named because it is 3.3mm long. Miyuki calls its similar bead a size 8º Delica. Both sizes of cylinder beads (11º and 8º) are also available as hex-cuts (**c**).

Choosing seed beads

People tend to favor one type of seed bead, but each type is better for some projects than for others. For example, if you want to achieve a traditional Native American look, Czech seed beads are the best choice. Today, Native Americans often use Japanese seed beads along with Czech beads in their non-traditional beadwork. In stitches where the beads meet each other end to end or side to side – peyote stitch, brick stitch, and square stitch, (**p. 12-15**), Japanese cylinder beads are often the first choice, especially if the beader wants her piece to have a smooth, flat surface. When a more textured surface is desired, Czech or round Japanese seed beads are preferable. For right-angle weave, in which groups of four or more beads form circular stitches, the rounder the seed bead, the better, so you aren't distracted by looking directly into a lot of bead holes. Round seed beads are also better for netting (**p. 16**) and strung jewelry (**p. 7**).

Threads for beadweaving

Beadweaving threads need to be strong and thin because they endure a lot of abrasion, and the bead hole must accept 2-4 (sometimes more) passes of thread. The two most popular and available threads are **Nymo, size B or D (a, photo above)**, and **Silamide (b)**, which comes in size A. (The earlier in the alphabet, the thinner the thread, except size O, which is thinner than A.) Both threads are nylon. Nymo is a filament thread, which means that long fibers of nylon run side by side. Silamide is a two-strand plied (twisted) thread and is used in the tailoring industry. Both come in many colors.

Nymo is easier to thread because it can be flattened; Silamide remains round. Both will build up twist that must be released periodically as you work. Because of their round vs. flat profiles, Silamide will fill bead holes with fewer passes than will Nymo B. If you want your beadwork to be stiff, this is important.

Other strong threads are also used by some beaders, though they're harder to find. **Kevlar**, the stuff used to make bullet-proof vests, is exceedingly strong; but it is slippery, and one strand can cut anoth-

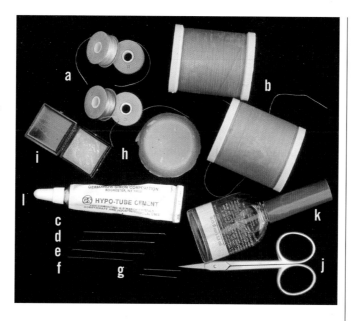

er when pulled across it. **Rod winding** is a filament thread that comes in many colors; it is used for making fishing equipment. **Fireline**, a fused polypropylene fishing fiber, is nearly unbreakable (use 4-6-lb. test). Never use cotton or poly-cotton sewing thread because it breaks easily.

Beading needles

Just like seed beads, the higher the number, the finer the beading needle. English beading needles are more flexible than Japanese needles. Unlike sewing needles, the eye area of a beading needle is almost as narrow as its shaft. If you work mostly with cylinder beads, you can use a thicker needle than is possible when weaving with Czech seed beads, which often don't accommodate the eye of a **size 10 (c)** needle. As you become comfortable with seed beads, you'll use **size 12 (d) or 13 (e)** needles. These are harder to thread but easier to use than size 10. **Size 15 or 16 (f)** needles are often necessary when using very small beads (vintage size 16°s or smaller). Size 16 needles are less fragile that 15s. For bead embroidery, you may prefer a

short needle such as a **size 12 between (g) or sharp.**

Thread conditioner

Most beaders usually pull their thread through a thread conditioner to strengthen it and reduce tangling and fraying (not necessary with silamide because it's already waxed). The best conditioners are **pure beeswax (h)** and **Thread Heaven (i)**, an acid-free, synthetic product that puts a static charge into the thread. It is excellent on single threads but doesn't work well on doubled threads, causing them to repel each other. Do not use candle wax, which contains hydrocarbons that weaken thread.

Scissors and glue

Small, sharp, pointed scissors such as Solingen steel **manicure scissors (j)** are ideal for trimming threads close. For sealing knots, most beaders apply a drop of **clear nail polish (k)** with the tip of the needle. **G-S Hypo Cement (l)**, a watch-crystal cement with an applicator shaped like a hypodermic needle, is even stronger. Do not seal knots with cyanoacrylate (Super) glue; it makes threads brittle.

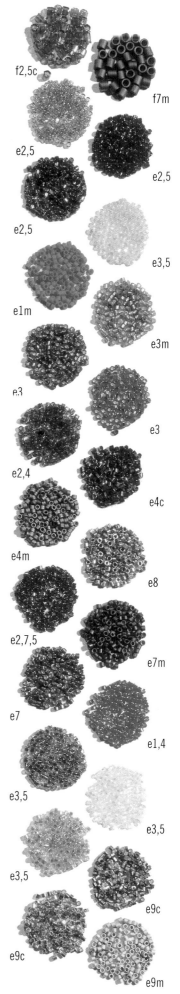

f2,5c
f7m
e2,5
e2,5
e2,5
e3,5
e1m
e3m
e3
e3
e2,4
e4c
e4m
e8
e2,7,5
e7m
e7
e1,4
e3,5
e3,5
e3,5
e9c
e9c
e9m

Stitches

With all beadweaving stitches, tension is the key to excellent results. For most projects, you'll want to weave with a gentle, even tension that results in a supple bead fabric. If you're tense or nervous, your tension will reflect it, and the beadwork will be stiff. However, for sculptural beadwork, you usually need to use the tightest tension you can manage.

Peyote stitch
Flat peyote stitch (even count)

Figure 1: String one bead and loop through it again in the same direction, leaving a 6-8-in. (15-20cm) tail. String more beads to total an even number. These beads comprise the first two rows. (As you weave, the beads of the new row will nestle into the spaces between the beads on the previous row. Remove the extra loop and weave the tail into the beadwork later.)

Figure 2: Every other bead from figure 1 drops down half a space to form row 1. To begin row 3 (count rows diagonally), pick up a bead and stitch through the second bead from the end. Pick up a bead and go through the fourth bead from the end. Continue in this manner. End by going through the first bead strung.

Figure 3: To start row 4 and all other rows, pick up a bead and go through the last bead added on the previous row.

End threads by weaving through the work in a zigzag path. Begin threads the same way, exiting the last bead added in the same direction.

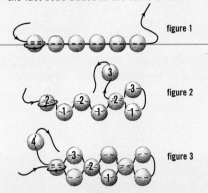

figure 1

figure 2

figure 3

Flat peyote stitch (odd count)

If the first two rows total an odd number of beads, you won't have a place to attach the last bead on odd-numbered rows. (The turn at the end of even-numbered rows is as shown in figure 3.)

Figure 4: Work a figure-8 turn at the end of row 3, which will position you to start row 4: String the next-to the last bead (#7) and go through #2, then #1. String the last bead (#8) and go through #2, #3, #7, #2, #1, and #8. You can continue to work this turn at the end of each odd-numbered row, but this edge will be noticeably stiffer than the other. Use either figure 5 or 6 to turn with a softer edge on subsequent odd-numbered rows.

Figure 5: String the last bead of the row, then loop through the edge thread immediately below. Go back through the last bead to begin the new row.

Figure 6: Work a modified turn to attach the last bead (#5): Exit #4, string #5. Go through #3, #2, #4, #3, and #5.

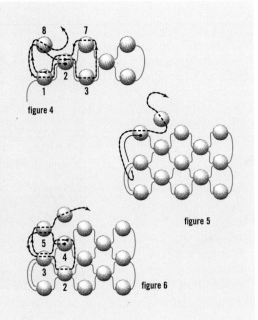

figure 4

figure 5

figure 6

Tubular peyote stitch

Figure 7: String beads to equal the desired circumference. Tie in a circle with enough slack for 2-3 more beads. Even-numbered beads form row 1 and odd-numbered beads make up row 2.

Figure 8: Slip the ring over a form. Go through the first bead to the left of the knot. Pick up a bead (#1 of row 3), skip a bead and go through the next bead. Repeat around until you're back to the start.

Figure 9: To begin each row if you started with an even number of beads, as shown, go through the first beads of rows 2 and 3. This is called the "step up," which positions you to start the next row. Pick up a bead and go through the second bead of row 3; repeat. Note: if you begin with an odd number of beads, there won't be a step up; you'll keep spiraling.

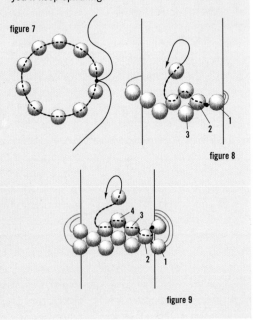

figure 7

figure 8

figure 9

The easiest way to do tubular peyote stitch is around a form. Woven with Japanese cylinder beads, this dramatic necklace goes quickly.

t

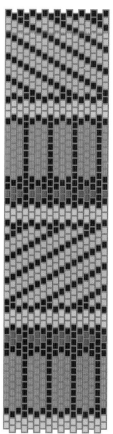

■ 010 black hex
▨ 029 metallic purple/gold iris
▨ 037 copper lined crystal
▨ 126 pink luster light olive
■ silver-lined copper

Project 8: Tubular peyote stitch choker

materials

- Delica beads, color #s: DB029, 037, 126, 601, and 010 hex-cut
- 24 in. (61cm) Plastic tubing, ¼ - in. (6mm) diameter (plumbing section in home repair store)
- Nymo B beading thread, black
- Thread Heaven or beeswax
- **2** 12 x 8mm Bronze accent beads
- 24 in. (61cm) Flexible beading wire
- 1-in. (2.5cm) Gold S-hook clasp
- 2 Gold crimp beads
- 2 Gold split rings, 5-6mm
- Beading needle, #13

Tools: crimping pliers, wire cutters, clear nail polish

stepbystep

❶ Measure your neck where you want the finished necklace to rest. Now subtract the length of both accent beads, the clasp, and ¼ in. (6mm) for the crimp beads. The remainder is the length of the peyote-covered tube.

❷ Cut a piece of plastic tubing the length calculated in step 1. With 40 in. (1m) of waxed thread, string 17 black Japanese cylinder beads, leaving a 6-in. (15cm) tail. Tie into a circle with a granny knot (**p. 19**). Slip the ring over the tube to check fit. Adjust the knot as needed, then secure it with a square knot. Following the **chart** at right, work tubular peyote stitch around the tube.

❸ When you reach the end of the tube, go through all the beads in the last row (**photo t**). Pull the thread tight to form a lip over the end of the tube. Go through the beads again. Then weave the thread back into the beadwork and secure it with two half hitches (**p. 19**). Seal each knot with polish. Go through 2-3 beads and trim.

❹ Thread a needle onto the starting tail. Go through all the beads in the first row and end as in step 3.

❺ Cut a piece of flexible beading wire the length of your finished necklace plus 6 in. (15cm). String a crimp bead and a split ring. Bring the wire tail back through the crimp and crimp it (**see p. 6, photos g and h**). String an accent bead, the peyote tube, an accent bead, a crimp bead, and the other split ring. Go back through the crimp bead again, pull up the slack, and crimp. Link the split rings in back with the S-hook. ●

Stitches
Earring: Project 9

Brick stitch looks like peyote stitch turned sideways. It is formed by weaving beads onto the thread loops between the beads on the previous row.

figure 1

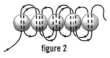

figure 2

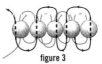

figure 3

figure 4

figure 5

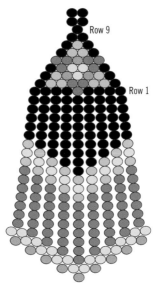

Row 9

Row 1

Brick stitch

Figure 1: Begin brick stitch with a ladder of seed or bugle beads. Pick up 2 beads. Leaving a 6-8-in. tail (15-20cm), go through both beads again in the same direction. Pull the top bead down so the beads sit side by side. The thread exits the bottom of the second bead. String bead #3 and go back through #2 from top to bottom. Come back up #3.

Figure 2: String bead #4. Go through #3 from bottom to top and #4 from top to bottom. Add odd-numbered beads like #3 and even-numbered beads like #4.

Figure 3: To stabilize the ladder, zigzag back through it.

Figure 4: Begin each brick stitch row so no thread shows on the edge as follows: String 2 seed beads. Go under the thread between the 2nd and 3rd beads on the ladder from back to front. Pull tight. Go up the 2nd bead added then down the first. Come back up the second bead again.

Figure 5: For the rest of each row, pick up 1 bead at a time. Pass the needle under the next loop on the row below from back to front and go back through the new bead. Brick stitch worked as in figures 4 and 5 will be triangular with each row 1 bead shorter than the one before.

Project 9:
Brick stitch earrings

materials

- Czech seed beads, size 11º: black, blue, orange, yellow, green
- Nymo B beading thread, black
- Beading needle, #12 or 13
- Pair of earring findings with a loop
- Clear nail polish

Tools: chainnose pliers

stepbystep

❶ Thread a beading needle with 40 in. (1m) of Nymo B. Start with row 1 on the **chart at left** and make a 9-bead ladder of 4 black, 1 blue, and 4 black beads (**see figures 1-3**). Select same-size beads.

❷ To begin row 2, pick up 1 black and 1 green bead and work as shown in **figure 4**. Work the rest of the row as **figure 5**, following the chart.

❸ Work through row 8.

❹ For row 9, pick up 1 black bead and reenter the other bead on row 8.

❺ Come back up the first row-8 bead and the row-9 bead and string 4 black beads for the loop. Go through the 5 top beads 1-2 more times to reinforce the loop.

❻ Exiting the row 9 bead, bring the needle diagonally down the side beads so it exits a bottom corner of row 1.

❼ Thread a needle onto the starting tail and weave it diagonally through two beads. Tie a half hitch (**p. 19**) and dot with clear nail polish. Weave through a few more beads and clip.

❽ For the first fringe, string 5 black, 1 green, 1 yellow, 1 green, 7 blue, 1 yellow, 1 orange, and 1 yellow. Skipping the last 3 beads to make a little florette on the end of the fringe, go back up all the fringe beads and the ladder bead you exited. To tighten the fringe, hold the orange bead and pull the thread taut (**photo u**). The fringe should be tight enough to prevent thread from showing but loose enough to hang softly.

❾ Bring the needle down the second ladder bead to start the second fringe, and string according to the chart. Notice that each fringe to the center has one more black bead. When all the fringes have been strung, end the thread in the beadwork as you did the tail.

❿ Use chainnose pliers to open the loop on an earring finding and hang the beadwork as shown above. ●

u

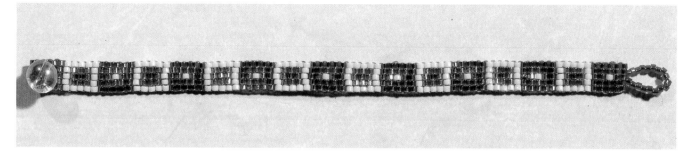

Project 10: Square stitch bracelet

materials

- Japanese cylinder beads: DB105 (gold luster transp. dark red)/047 (silver-lined sapphire); 355 (matte rose)/111 (gray luster AB); 82 (lined pink AB)/211 (opaque alabaster luster)
- Light brown Silamide or blue Nymo B
- Beading needle, #12 or 13
- ⅜-in. (1cm) Shank button

stepbystep

❶ Begin with 2 yd. (1.8m) of thread, and tie a stop bead 24 in. (61cm) from the end (**figure 1**).

❷ String the 5 dark-colored beads of row 1. Then follow **figure 2** and the **chart** to stitch a dark bead, 3 medium beads, and a dark bead onto the row 1 beads one at a time.

❸ Begin row 3 as in **figure 3** and work through row 10. To keep the rows straight and square, after every few rows, run the needle back through all the beads on the previous row then through all the beads on the last row.

❹ Repeat rows 1-10 until

the bracelet is about ⅜ in. (1cm) short of the total desired length. End with rows 1-5.

❺ Before squaring the last three rows, double the thread by pulling the tail through the needle so it is a little longer than the remaining thread. Go back through the next-to-last row and the row before that. Then come back through the next-to-last row and the first two beads of the last row (**photo v**).

❻ String enough beads for the button loop to go around the button. Then skip the center bead of the last row and go through the last 2 beads (**photo w**). Reinforce the loop by going through the next-to-last row, the last row, and the loop again. End the thread by weaving back through the beadwork.

❼ At the starting end, take off the stop bead and double the thread as in step 5. Weave back through the beadwork to exit the light bead in the middle of the first square. Sew on the button (**photo x**) and reinforce as much as the bead holes will allow. End as in step 6. ●

Square stitch

Square stitch looks like loom weaving but is done without a loom.

Figure 1: If desired, tie a temporary stop bead on the thread 4-6 in. (10-15cm) from the end. String the number of beads for the width of the piece.

Figure 2. To weave the second row, string 1 bead and place it directly above the last bead on the first row. Bring the needle through the last bead of row 1 and the first bead of row 2 in the same direction. Repeat this step one bead at a time above each bead on row 1.

Figure 3: Work row 3 exactly like row 2, but start at the other side. Turn the work over as needed for comfort.

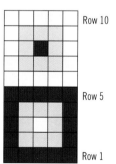

x

Stitches
Bracelet: Project 10

This easy square stitch bracelet takes less than three hours. Make it with three shades of any color, dark, medium, and light.

figure 1

figure 2

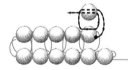

figure 3

Row 10

Row 5

Row 1

■ 105/047 Dark

□ 355/111 Medium

□ 82/211 Light

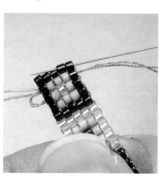

v

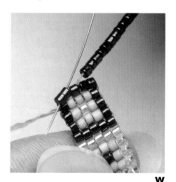

w

Netting is an easy loop
stitch that makes a
lacy fabric.

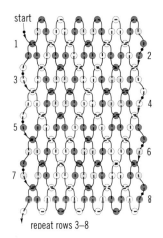

start
1
2
3
4
5
6
7
8

repeat rows 3–8

Project 11: Netted rose trellis bracelet

materials

- 3g Seed beads, size 11º in each of 4 colors: off-white (W), dark pink (D), light pink (L), green (G)
- Bead thread, Nymo D or Silamide
- Beading needles, # 12
- 1 Small button or 1 8mm beaded bead (p. 9)

stepbystep

❶ Cut a 4-yd. (3.6m) thread and slide a needle to the middle to double it. String 2 times through a stop bead 4 in. (10cm) from the end.

❷ For row 1, string 24 beads in the colors shown on the chart: D, L, D; *G, 5W, G, D*; L, D, L, D; repeat *-* and end L. For the turning bead, string 1 D.

❸ Follow the chart from right to left for row 2. String G, 2 W and go through the last W bead on row 1; G, D,

G (from now on, skip 3 on row 1 and go through the 4th bead after stringing each 3-bead group); 2W, G*; repeat *-*. Turn with G, W.

❹ Repeat step 3 for each consecutive row through row 8, following the pattern. If you have trouble reading the chart, follow rows 3-8 below:
Row 3: 3W; G, D, L; L, D, G; repeat; turn 2W
Row 4: 2W, G; L, D, L; G, 2W; repeat; turn 2W
Row 5: G, D, G; 2W, G; G, 2W; repeat; turn G, DP
Row 6: L, D, G; 3 W; G, D, L; repeat; turn L, D
Row 7: L, D, L; G, 2W; 2W, G; repeat; turn L, D
Row 8: G, 2W; G, D, G; 2W, G; repeat; turn G, W
❺ Repeat rows 3-8 until the bracelet is your wrist mea-

y

z

aa

bb

Horizontal flat netting

Netting is woven by making loops of beads with an odd number of beads in each loop. You string the number of beads for a net stitch, then go through the center bead of the loop on the row above. In flat netting, you need to add extra beads at the row ends to keep the edges flat.

Row 1: For flat, even-count netting, the first row of stitches includes 1 extra bead per stitch (the points at the top of the row – here 4 beads for 3-bead nets). There is also 1 extra bead for turning to row 2.

Row 2: String an odd number of beads, here 3, and go through the fifth bead from the end of row 1. For the rest of the row, string 3, skip 3 on row 1, and go through the 4th bead until you've gone through the first bead on row 1.

Row 3: From now on, string 2 turning beads. Then string 3 and go through the middle bead of the last 3-bead group on the previous row. Note: for 5-bead nets, you would string 3 turning beads; for 7-bead nets, 4; and so on.

surement plus ½ in. (1.3cm).

❻ When your thread is about 6 in. (15cm) long, thread a new needle with doubled thread and knot the ends. Insert the new needle about 2 stitches back from the last stitch and go through all 3 beads of the net. Tie a half hitch (p. 19) around the thread. Repeat. When both needles exit the same bead, tie the threads together with a square knot (photo y and p. 19). Resume beading with the new thread. Then weave the old thread through a few stitches on previous rows, tying at least 2 half hitches. Go through a few beads before cutting the old thread.

❼ To finish the bracelet, sew an 8mm beaded bead (p. 9) or a small button between the two center points: Weave and knot a new doubled thread into the bracelet and exit the first net bead on one side of the center, pointing toward the edge. String 2 seed beads, go through the bead or button, and come through 1 bead at the top hole. String 1-3 seed beads and go through a bead opposite the first edge bead (photo z). Then go down the beaded bead, through the first stem bead, and string 1 seed bead. Go into the first net bead on the other side of the center (photo aa). Weave and knot the thread into the bracelet.

❽ Add a new thread at the other end of the bracelet, centering it about 10 rows from the edge. String a loop of seed beads between 2 net beads to correspond to the button placement. Make the loop just long enough to fit over the bead or button (photo bb). Go through the loop again to reinforce it. Then weave the thread securely into the bracelet. ◉

Project 12: Beaded bead necklace

materials

- **5-9** Wooden beads with large holes (14-20mm)
- **1** Large-hole wooden bead, 10-12mm, or shank button
- **1-5** Coordinating colors of seed beads, size 11º, 3-7g each
- **4-12** Coordinating-color fancy yarns and thin ribbons, 2 yd. (1.8m) each piece
- **5 yd. (4.6m)** Smooth yarn or waxed linen cord
  2 or more Thin tapestry needles

stepbystep

❶ Make an odd number of large beaded beads (p. 9) on 14-20mm wooden beads or larger. Make 2 of each size

except the largest (make one for the center).

❷ Collect a variety of flashy yarns and narrow ribbons and cut them into 2-yd. (1.8m) lengths. Thread the yarns on one or more tapestry needles at each end.

❸ Thread the largest beaded bead to the center of the group of yarns and tie a fat overhand knot (p. 19) about ½-1 in. (1.3-2.5cm) from each side of the bead (photo cc). (Hint: If a disaster occurs as you're stringing the beads and one of the seed bead threads breaks, immediately coat the seed beads around both ends of the break heavily with clear nail polish.)

❹ Thread one each of the next largest bead on each end

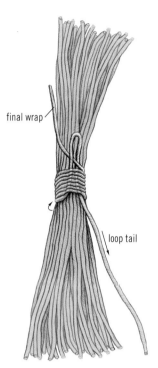

final wrap

loop tail

cc

of the yarns and slide them close to the knots. Knot after each as in step 3.

❺ Repeat step 4 for all the beaded beads, graduating to the smallest size.

❻ Leave plain yarn for the upper sides and back portion of the necklace. You can tie overhand spaced knots in this section if you wish.

❼ Make a smaller beaded bead (10-12mm) or use a shank button for the clasp.

❽ Bring 3-4 of the smooth yarns and ribbons through the button or small beaded bead. If using a bead, knot outside the hole. Then carry the yarns back through the bead (**photo dd**).

❾ Take 1 yd. (.9m) of smooth yarn, ribbon, or waxed linen and lash around the last ½-1 in. of all the yarns below the button bead (**figure, p. 17**). Then trim the yarn and ribbon tails.

❿ For the loop, wind a smooth yarn or ribbon tightly around 3-4 smooth yarns for a length long enough to make a loop that will fit over the button. Fold the tails

dd

ee

back against the unwrapped ribbons and yarns toward the beads and wrap around all the ribbons and yarns for ½-1 in. (**photo ee**). Use a tapestry needle to feed the tail of the wrapping yarn back under the wraps (**photo ff**). Then cut off all the tails. ◉

ff

gg

hh

ii

jj

Stitches
Ring: Project 13

Easy square-knot macramé requires four cords. You tie the two outer cords around the two inner ones to create a flat, knotted band good for necklaces, bracelets, and even rings.

figure 1   figure 2

Project 13: Macramé ring

A ring of macramé square knots with a bead centerpiece takes almost no time to make. The key is to make sure that four cords will pass through the bead.

materials

- 1 Large-hole bead or a shank button
- 1½ yd. (1.4m) Waxed linen cord or hemp

Tools: Scissors; white glue optional

stepbystep

❶ Cut the cord into two 21-in. (53cm) lengths and one 12-in. (30cm) length.

❷ Center the 12-in. cord in the bead and loop it through the bead again so it forms a ring with one end on each side of the hole (**photo gg**). Make the ring bigger than the desired finished size.

❸ Center the other two cords through the bead, one on each side of the ring cord.

❹ Using the two long ends on one side of the ring, tie 8-12 square knots alternating **figures 1 and 2** over the ring and the end on that side of the bead (**photo hh**).

❺ Turn the bead ring over and pull the cord ring so the knots are against the hole or shank. Tie 8-12 square knots with the other pair of ends

around the other side of the ring (**photo ii**).

❻ Try the ring on your finger. It must fit loosely over the largest knuckle because the knots will thicken the band. If it is very loose, pull one of the cord ring tails to make the circle smaller.

❼ When you only need about 4 more knots, bend the ring tail and knotting ends from one side toward the side that you'll use to finish knotting and knot over all the cord thicknesses (**photo jj**).

❽ Pull the last knot very tight and cut off all the tails. If you're using hemp, dot the final knot with white glue. ◉